NIGHT of the CRASH-TEST DUMMIES

Other Books in The Far Side Series from Futura

The Far Side
Beyond The Far Side
In Search of The Far Side
Bride of The Far Side
Valley of The Far Side
Hound of The Far Side
It Came from The Far Side
The Far Side Gallery
The Far Side Gallery 2
The Far Side Observer

NIGHT of the CRASH-TEST DUMMIES

A Far Side Collection
by Gary Larson

Futura

A Futura Book

Copyright © 1988 by Universal Press Syndicate

First published in Great Britain in 1989 by Futura Publications,
a Division of Macdonald & Co (Publishers) Ltd
London & Sydney

ISBN 0 7088 4455 3

Printed in Great Britain by
The Guernsey Press Co. Ltd, Guernsey, Channel Islands.

Futura Publications
A Division of
Macdonald & Co (Publishers) Ltd
66-73 Shoe Lane
London EC4P 4AB

A member of Maxwell Pergamon Publishing Corporation plc

NIGHT of the CRASH-TEST DUMMIES

Animal Camouflage

The rural professional and his cowphone

"Oh, wonderful! Look at this, Etta — another mouth to feed."

"For crying out loud, I was *hibernating*! ... Don't you guys ever take a pulse?"

"He told you *that*? Well, he's pulling your flagellum, Nancy."

"Hey, bucko ... I'm *through* begging."

9

"Hey, Johnny! This lady wants to know the difference in all these fertilizers!"

Through some unfortunate celestial error, Ernie is sent to Hog Heaven.

The Bluebird of Happiness long absent from his life, Ned is visited by the Chicken of Depression.

"Oh my God! It's from Connie! She's written me a 'John deer' letter!"

11

"So! Planning on roaming the neighborhood with some of your buddies today?"

"And *you*, Johnson! You stick with your man and keep that hand in his *face!*"

Single-cell bars

Where beef jerky comes from

"Now go to sleep, Kevin — or once again I'll have to knock three times and summon the Floating Head of Death."

14

"Ah, yes, Mr. Frischberg, I thought you'd come ... but which of us is the *real* duck, Mr. Frischberg, and not just an illusion?"

That evening, with her blinds pulled, Mary had three helpings of corn, two baked potatoes, extra bread, and a little lamb.

"No, wait! *That's* not Uncle Floyd! Who is that? ...
Criminy, I think it's just an air bubble!"

Bird cellars

16

"Hold it right there, Henry! ... You ain't plannin' on takin' that wrinkled horse into town, are you?"

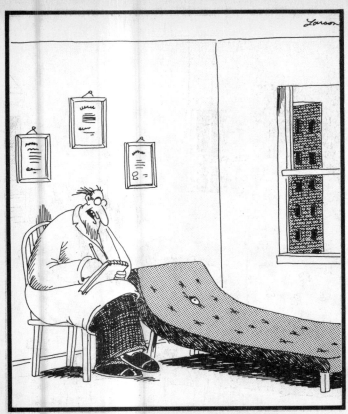

"Frankly, you've got a lot of anger toward
the world to work out, Mr. Pembrose."

Suddenly, throwing the festivities into utter
confusion, Ujang begins to play "Stardust."

19

School for the Mechanically Declined

The Lone Ranger, long since retired, makes an unpleasant discovery.

Where we get fat

At the Vincent van Gogh School of Art

"Oh, my! Aren't *these* fancy drinks!"

"Say, Will — why don't you pull that
thing out and play us a tune?"

...but the Secretary of State declined
to comment on the latest round of talks...
...And today the A-1 Life Raft Co. issued
a statement recalling 50,000 of its small
rubber boats due to defective glue used
in their manufacture, causing the boats to
lose air and gradually sink over a matter
of a few days...
And now let's go to Lou Jackson
for what's happening in sports...

The famous "Mr. Ed. vs. Francis the Talking Mule" debates

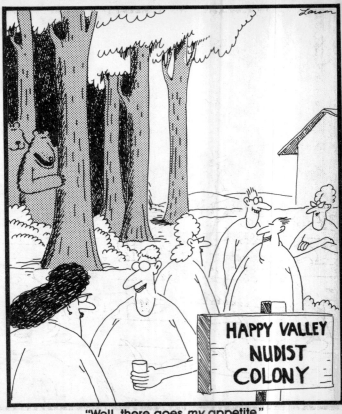

HAPPY VALLEY NUDIST COLONY

"Well, there goes *my* appetite."

"So then, when Old MacDonald turned his back, I took that ax, and with a whack whack here and a whack whack there, I finished him off."

"Ernie! Look what you're doing — take those shoes off!"

26

Secret tools of the common crow

The townsfolk all stopped and stared;
they didn't know the tall stranger who
rode calmly through their midst, but they
did know the reign of terror had ended.

"Bob and Ruth! Come on in. ... Have you
met Russell and Bill, our 1.5 children?"

28

The Potatoheads in Paris

"Johnson, back off! It's an *Armandia lidderdalii*, all right — but it's rabid!"

"Well, let's see. . . . So far I've got rhythm and
I've got music . . . actually, who could ask
for anything more?"

"Beats me how they did it ... I got the
whole thing at a garage sale for five
bucks — and that included the stand."

Embarrassing moments at gene parties

Fruitcases

In the Fly House of Horrors

When ornithologists are mutually attracted

"That's a lie, Morty! ... Mom says you might have got the brains in the family, but *I* got the looks!"

Night of the Potato Bugs

How fishermen blow their own minds

Although troubled as a child, Zorro, as is well known, ultimately found his niche in history.

And then, just as he predicted, Thag became the channeler for a two million-year-old gibbon named Gus.

Sled chickens of the North

Jazz at the Wool Club

What really happened to Elvis

"Anytime, Slim."

Rocking the anthropological world, a second
"Lucy" is discovered in southern Uganda.

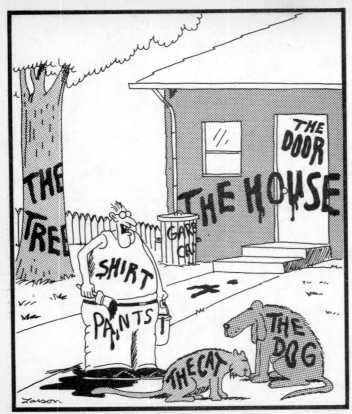

"Now! ... *That* should clear up
a few things around here!"

Cartoon readings

The committee to decide whether spawning should be taught in school

"Green blood? I *hate* green blood."

Baryshnikov's ultimate nightmare

All day long, a tough gang of astrophysicists
would monopolize the telescope and intimidate
the other researchers.

At the popular dog film, *Man Throwing Sticks*

"Mind? Hey, buddy, these flat feet kept me out of the Army!"

Metamorphosis Nightclubs

The squid family on vacation

"Clean it up? Clean it up? Criminy, it's *supposed* to be a rathole!"

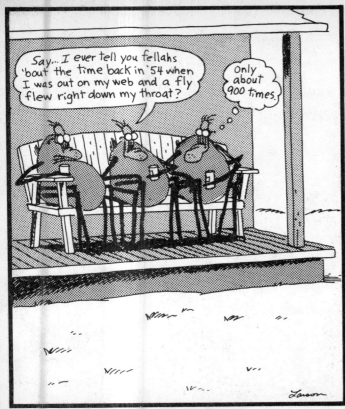

At the Old Spiders' Home

Rusty makes his move.

"Hey, I'm not *crazy* ... sure, I let him drive once in a while, but he's never, *never* off this leash for even a second."

"Mom! The kids at school say we're a family of Nerdenthals! ... Is that true?"

48

When chickens dream

"OK. I'll go back and tell my people that you're staying in the boat, but I warn you they're *not* going to like it."

But your pipe was found at the scene, sir! We know you did it!... Have you no remorse? What kind of monster are you?

I yam what I yam.

Full moon and empty head

Just as Dale entered the clearing and discovered, standing together, the Loch Ness monster, Bigfoot, and Jackie Onassis, his camera jammed.

51

Hell's library

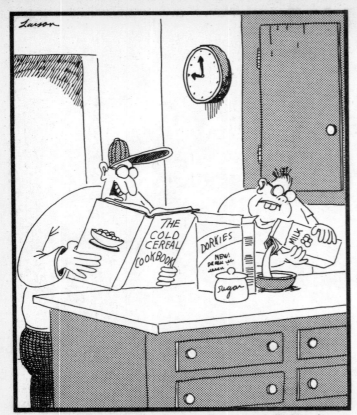

"Oh, wait! Wait, Cory! ... Add the cereal *first* and
then the milk!"

Early microbiologists

With their parents away, the young dragons would stay up late lighting their sneezes.

"Well, down I go."

Piglet practical jokes

"Hey, you wanna see a *real* scar? Check *this* baby out!"

"Well, the defendant and I had made this
deal in which we both prospered. ...
One of those 'you-scratch-me-behind-my-ears-
I'll-scratch-you-behind-yours' arrangements."

"Oh, don't be silly! No thanks needed.
Just take the brain — but tell that doctor
you work for not to be such a stranger."

Parakeet furniture

Man, this place is great... I tell you, I can come down from the hills, stand on this corner, and just feel myself unwind.

How bears relax

Canine comedians

"It's a letter from Julio in America. ...
His banana bunch arrived safely and he's
living in the back room of some grocery store."

Nerds in hell

"Here are the blueprints. Now look: This is going to be the *Liberty* Bell, so we obviously expect that it be forged with great diligence and skill."

"When I got home, Harold's coat and hat were gone, his worries were on the doorstep, and Gladys Mitchell, my neighbor, says she saw him heading west on the sunny side of the street."

63

Songwriters of the Old West

"Listen. I've *tried* to communicate with him, but he's like a broken record: 'None of your bee's wax, none of your bee's wax.'"

Punk flamingoes

"Drive, George, drive! This one's got a coat hanger!"

"What the hey? ... Someone's shortsheeted my bed again!"

"Tough break, Rusty. ... Seven years bad luck — of course, in your case, that works out to 49 years."

Another unsubstantiated photograph of the Loch Ness monster (taken by Reuben Hicks, 5/24/84, Chicago)

Impolite as they were, the other bears could never help staring at Larry's enormous deer gut.

"Oh, boy! The 'Nerd'! ... Now my collection's complete!"

69

"It's the same dream night after night ...
I walk out on my web, and suddenly a foot
sticks — and then another foot sticks, and
another, and another, and another ..."

"A few cattle are going to stray off in the morning,
and tomorrow night a stampede is planned around
midnight. Look, I gotta get back. ... Remember,
when we reach Santa Fe, I ain't slaughtered."

Dial-a-Cat

"Well, the sloth nailed him ... y'know,
ol' Hank never was exactly a 'quick draw.'"

"Blow, Howie, blow! ... Yeah, yeah, yeah!
You're cookin' now, Howie! ... All right! ...
Charlie Parker, move over! ... Yeah!"

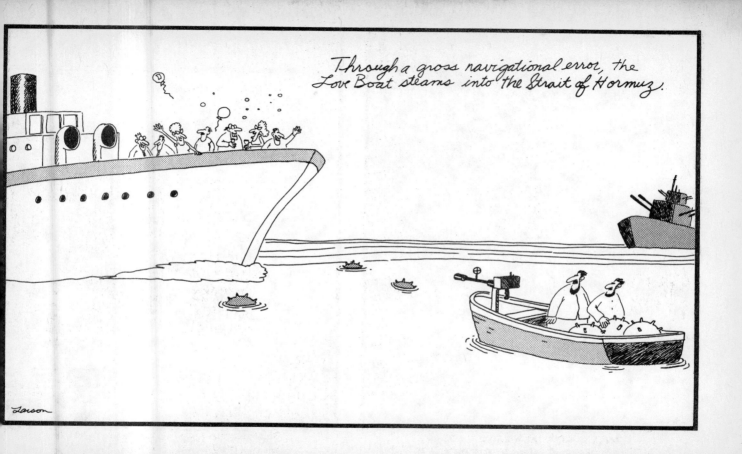

Through a gross navigational error, the Love Boat steams into the Strait of Hormuz.

"Hey, Norton! ... Ain't that your dog attackin' the president?"

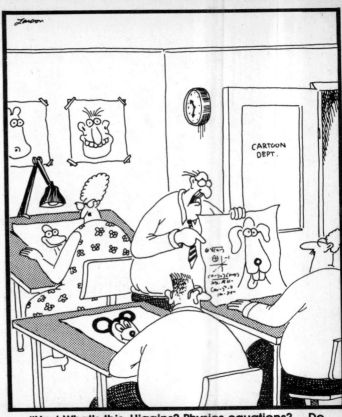

"Hey! What's this, Higgins? Physics equations? ... Do you enjoy your job here as a cartoonist, Higgins?"

"For crying out loud, Warren ... Can't you just
beat your chest like everyone else?"

Where all the young farm animals go to smoke

"Do I like it? Do I *like* it? ... Dang it, Thelma, you know my feelings on barbed wire."

Crow kids

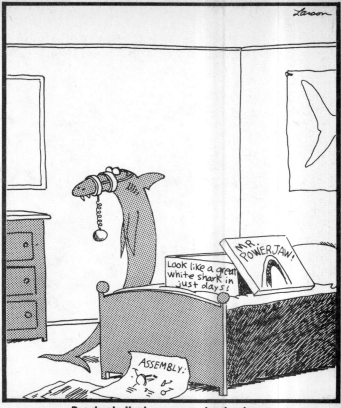

Products that prey on shark wimps

Killer bees are generally described
as starting out as larvae delinquents.

"Indians!"

Ornithology 101 field trips

Mutants on the *Bounty*

Wildlife preserves

"More worms? ... Saaaaaaaaay — why are you being so nice to me all of a sudden?"

How cow documentaries are made

"Vince! Just trample him! ... He's drawing
you into his kind of fight!"

"Yes! Yes! That's it! ... Just a little higher."

83

Mr. Ed spills his guts.

"Well, this is getting nowhere fast."

When piranha dine out

"Well, if I'm lucky, I should be able to get off this thing in about six more weeks."

"Again? You just had a
glass of water 12 days ago."

*I don't believe you heard
me right, stranger... I said
I'd like to buy you
a chicken leg!*

In the Old West, vegetarians were
often shot with little provocation.

"Won't talk, huh? ... Frankie! Hand me that scaler."

"This is it, Jenkins. ... Indisputable proof that the Ice Age caught these people completely off guard."

When jellyfish travel at unsafe speeds

"Shoot! Drain's clogged. ... Man, I hate
to think what might be down there."

"Now this is ... this is ... well,
I guess it's another snake."

"Oh my God! ... Murray's attacking
the bathroom mirror!"

"And so you just threw everything together?
... Mathews, a posse is something
you have to *organize*."

Animal horoscopes

Anthro horror films

Omelettes Etc.

Humpty Dumpty's final days

Java man

Peking man

Cro-Magnon man

Jazz man

Hominid reconstructions

"You know, it was supposed to be just a story about a little kid and a wolf . . . but off and on, I've been dressing up as a grandmother ever since."

"Now open even wider, Mr. Stevens. . . . Just out of curiosity, we're going to see if we can also cram in this tennis ball."

Suddenly, through forces not yet fully understood, Darren Belsky's apartment became the center of a new black hole.

"And when the big moment comes, here's the nursery Robert and I have fixed up."

Kangaroo nerds

The conversation had been brisk and pleasant when, suddenly and simultaneously, everyone just got dog tired.

"You're sick, Jessy! ... Sick, sick, sick!"

"For God's sake, hurry, driver! ... She's dropping babies all over the place!"

Cat showers

"Oh my gosh, Linda! ... I think your
Barbie's contemplating suicide!"

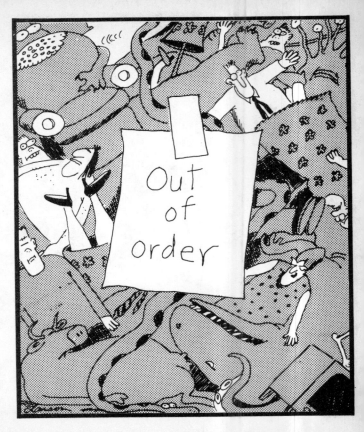

Futura now offers an exciting range of quality fiction and non-fiction by both established and new authors.
All of the books in this series are available from good bookshops, or can be ordered from the following address:

Futura Books
Cash Sales Department
P.O. Box 11
Falmouth
Cornwall, TR10 9EN.

Please send cheque or postal order (no currency), and allow 60p for postage and packing for the first book plus 25p for the second book and 15p for each additional book ordered up to a maximum charge of £1.50 in U.K.

B.F.P.O. customers please allow 60p for the first book, 25p for the second book plus 15p per copy for the next 7 books, thereafter 9p per book.

Overseas customers, including Eire, please allow £1.25 for postage and packing for the first book, 75p for the second book and 28p for each subsequent title ordered.